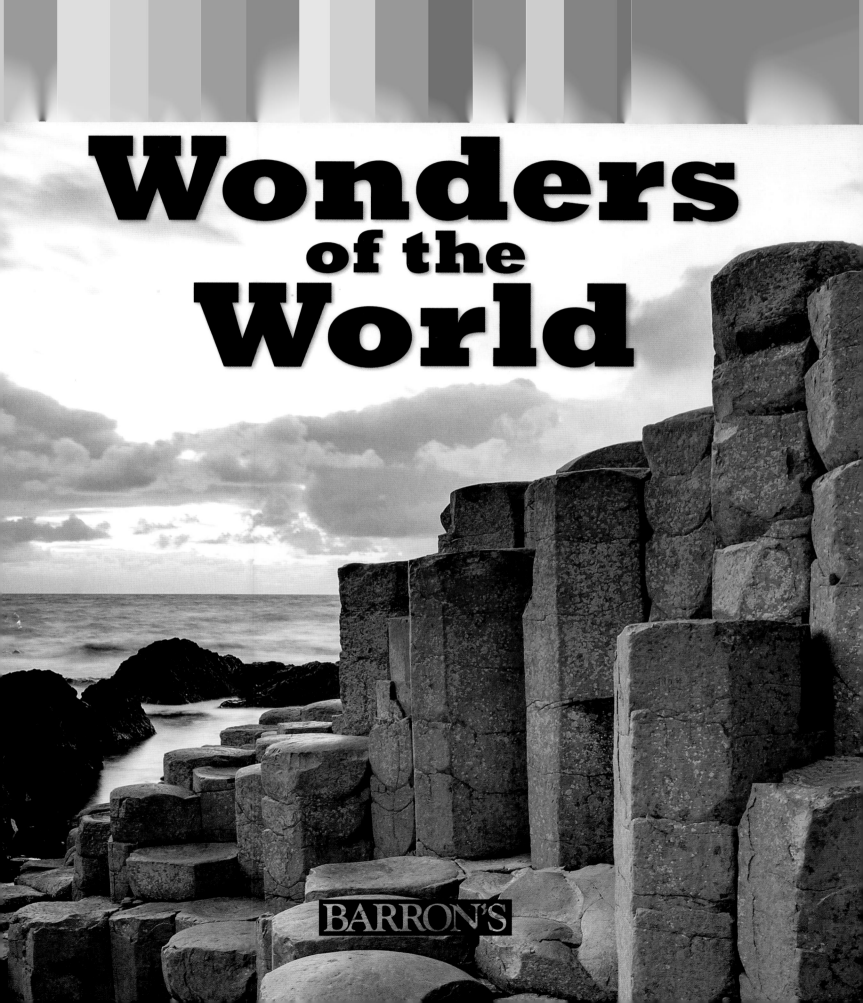

Wonders
of the
World

BARRON'S

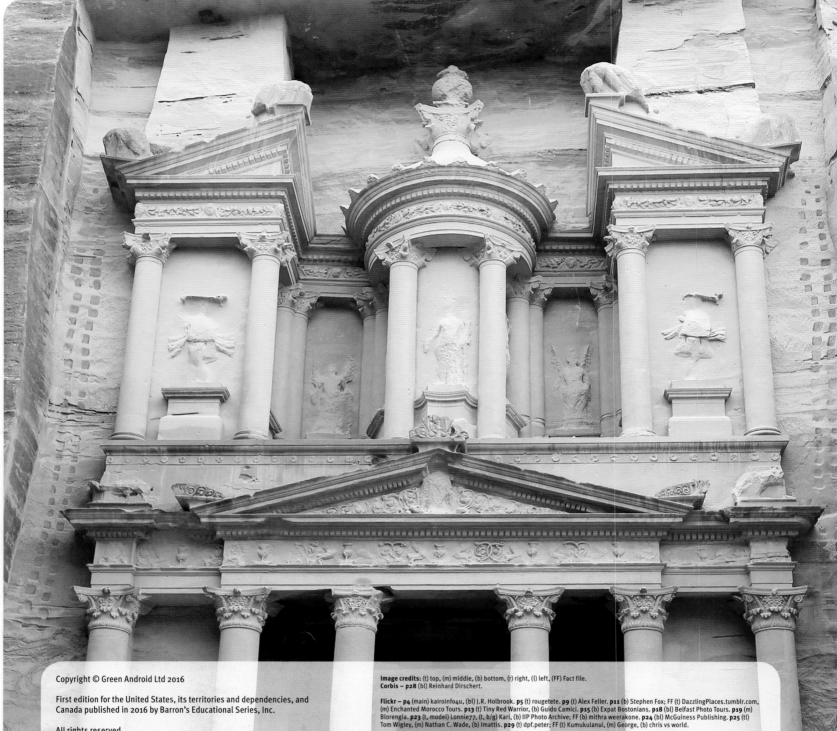

First edition for the United States, its territories and dependencies, and
Canada published in 2016 by Barron's Educational Series, Inc.

All inquiries should be addressed to:
Barron's Educational Series, Inc.
250 Wireless Boulevard
Hauppauge, NY 11788
www.barronseduc.com

ISBN: 978-1-4380-0830-1
Library of Congress Control Number: 2015956070

Date of Manufacture: January 2016
Manufactured by: Toppan Leefung Printing Co., Ltd., China

9 8 7 6 5 4 3 2 1

Image credits: (t) top, (m) middle, (b) bottom, (r) right, (l) left, (FF) Fact file.
Corbis – p28 (bl) Reinhard Dirschert.

Flickr – p4 (main) kairoinfo4u, (bl) J.R. Holbrook. **p5** (t) rougetete. **p9** (t) Alex Feller. **p11** (b) Stephen Fox; FF (t) DazzlingPlaces.tumblr.com,
(m) Enchanted Morocco Tours. **p13** (t) Tiny Red Warrior, (b) Guido Camici. **p15** (b) Expat Bostonians. **p18** (bl) Belfast Photo Tours. **p19** (m)
Blorengia. **p23** (t, model) Lonnie77, (t, b/g) Kari, (b) IIP Photo Archive; FF (b) mithra weerakone. **p24** (bl) McGuiness Publishing. **p25** (tl)
Tom Wigley, (m) Nathan C. Wade, (b) Imattis. **p29** (t) dpf.peter; FF (t) Kumukulanui, (m) George, (b) chris vs world.

FLPA – p9 (b) Fabio Pupin.

Getty – p7 (t) Digital Globe/Scapeware3D. **p9** De Agostini Picture Library. **p19** (b) Chris Hill; **p31** (t) Roger Viollet Collection.

iStock – p28 (main) itos.

Shutterstock – FC (main) Francesco R. Iacomino; (l–r) Aleksei Potov, feiyuezhangjie, apdesign, Dmitri Ometsinsky. Spine: Morozov67.
BC (l–r) 3523studio, tororo reaction, qingqing, Neil Burton. **p1** Aitormmfoto. **p2-3** VLADJ55. **p5** (m) Leonid Andronov, (b) Elena Terletskaya;
FF (t–b) Guzel Studio, Galyna Andrushko, Daniel Loncarevic. **p6** (main) Daniel Prudek, (bl) 360b. **p7** (m) Jun Mu, (b) contax66. **p8** (main)
Roberto Caucino, (bl) MarcelClemens. **p9** FF (t–b) Armin Rose, Claudiovidri, Guido Amrein, Switzerland. **p10** (main) Dietmar Temps,
(bl) e2dan. **p11** (t) 2630ben, (m) Vadim Petrakov, (b) Gil.K. **p12** (main) Robert Hoetink/Shutterstock.com, (bl) Oleg Znamenskiy. **p13** (m)
Nickolay Vinokurov. **p14** (main) Pius Lee. **p15** (tl) Marcel Toung, (tr) Arena Photo UK, (m) saiko3p; FF (t–b) pio3, Hung Chung Chih, Evgeniy
Agarkov. **p16** (main) Nadezhda Kulikova, (bl) aragami12345s. **p17** (t) Curioso, (m) chris kolaczan, (b) R.M. Nunes. **p18** (main) Aitormmfoto.
p19 (t) Claudio Rossoi; FF (t–b) Steve Bower, Spumador, Evgeny Gorodetsky. **p20** (main) kojihirano, (bl) turtix. **p21** (t) Gary Whitton,
(m) IgorColovniov, (b) Doug Meek; FF (t–b) Isabella Pfenninger, sigurcamp, Tim Stirling. **p22** (main) Joseph Sohm, (bl) Everett Historical.
p23 (ml, mr)) Everett Historical; FF (t) Sanchai Kurmar, (m) lazyllama. **p24** (main) sunsinger. **p26** (main) Kjersti Joergensen, (bl) AridOcean.
p27 (t) Rangzen, (b) Ben Queenborough; FF (t–b) M Reel, robert cicchetti, javarman. **p29** (m) Trent Townsend. **p30** (main) Pichugin Dmitry,
(bl) Fabio Lamanna. **p31** (ml) Ben Jeayes, (mr) smileimage9, (b) Karin Wassmer; FF (t–b) Edward Fielding, Vadim Petrakov, Aoshi VN.
p32 Jixin YU.

Introduction

Our planet is extraordinary. It is unique! It has awe-inspiring natural environments from arid deserts, reefs and islands teeming with life, tumbling waterfalls, and jets of boiling water coming straight from the Earth's molten heart. But equal in majesty are those places hewn from rock hundreds or thousands of years ago by humankind to honor a belief, a love, or to assure a ruler safe passage to the next life. Natural or man-made, these wondrous places will take your breath away.

Contents

Read on to marvel at natural and built wonders...

Great Pyramid of Giza

For centuries, people have **marveled** at the majestic Great Pyramid. It stands near Cairo, by the River **Nile** and the Western Desert, and is the only **ancient** wonder that still stands. Khufu's pyramid is the largest of the pyramids in the Giza **Necropolis**. The complex **construction** took more than 20 years, and was finished in 2560 BCE by **Egyptian** citizens who had to work for the **pharaoh** when flooding of the Nile prevented them from **farming**. At that time, the pyramid would have been even more impressive, surrounded by many **temples** and smaller pyramids.

Facts and figures

Cultural importance
The ancient ruins of the area were collectively designated a World Heritage Site in 1979.

The king's coffin
The king's solid granite coffin was placed in the pyramid before it was finished. It was too large for the passage to the burial chamber.

Massive monument
The Great Pyramid is estimated to weigh 6.5 million tons.

Granite blocks
The Great Pyramid is made up of about 2.3 million blocks.

Heavy lifting
The largest stone blocks weigh between 25–90 tons.

Towering wonder
The Great Pyramid was 480 ft (146 m) high, but it is now 450 ft (138 m). It was the tallest man-made structure in the world for more than 3,800 years.

Did you know?

The Orion correlation theory was first published by Robert Bauval in 1989. It suggests that the layout of the Giza pyramids was planned to match up with the three stars of Orion's Belt.

This **pyramid** tomb for **Khufu** prepared his **body** for the **journey** to the **afterlife**.

Golden capstone

Originally, the pyramid was almost 32 ft (10 m) taller, with a tip of gold. This was seen as the most important part of the pyramid.

Casing stones

When it was completed, the Great Pyramid was encased in highly-polished white limestone. Today we only see the stepped stones that would have been underneath.

The Great Pyramid is also called the Pyramid of Khufu, which was the name of the pharaoh for whom it was built.

Ancient ingenuity

The pyramids were built with accuracy and without sophisticated tools. The four corners of the bases align with the compass points at almost perfect right angles, and it is thought that the blocks were cut with copper saws, with sand being poured into the cuts to make the saw "bite" into the granite.

The granite was transported from nearby quarries

The Great Sphinx minus its 3-ft-wide nose

An artist's impression of the Colossus of Rhodes

The Great Sphinx

This limestone statue stands close to the Great Pyramid, and has the body of a lion and the face of a man. No one can be certain when it was built, or why, but it is most likely to be a guardian of the tombs. It wears a royal headdress, and would once have been covered in plaster and painted red.

Seven wonders

In ancient times, several places were seen as perfect by the Romans and Greeks. All these ancient wonders have disappeared, apart from the Great Pyramid. We can only imagine how they would have looked. UNESCO World Heritage Sites are the modern equivalents of those ancient places.

The Great Wall of China

The **biggest** structure built by man stretches thousands of miles through many different **terrains**, from the beaches at the coast to **desert** country, marshes, and mountains. It began as a series of individual walls intended to **protect** China from attack by **invaders**, and is made of stone, brick, earth, and wood, as well as other materials. The 17th-century **Ming** Dynasty wall, constructed in the final period of **building**, stretched 5,500 miles (8,800 km) across northern **China**. Although the wall fulfilled its function, it fell into disrepair due to the massive **expense** to maintain it.

Facts and figures

Engineering feat
In 1987, the Great Wall was designated a World Heritage Site.

Great length
Early estimates had the Great Wall at 4,000 miles (6,400 km) long, but with its offshoots the wall is around 13,000 miles (21,000 km) long.

Long history
Qin Shi Huang's wall was built between 220 and 206 BCE.

Lookouts
There are more than 10,000 watch towers on the Great Wall.

Preservation
Many areas of the wall are in need of repair, and 22 percent of the Ming Dynasty wall has toppled or disappeared.

Visible from space?
The wall is often described as the only man-made object visible from space, but this is a myth.

The exact length of the wall had to be estimated because many sections were located in remote areas

Strength and defense

The top of the wall is wide enough for 10 foot soldiers or five cavalry soldiers. Its defensive capabilities included watch towers, barracks, and garrison stations.

Worked to death

About 300,000 soldiers and many thousands of peasants and rebels were forced to work on the wall. The dead were buried in the wall.

Did you know?

The wall built by Qin Shi Huang, the first Emperor of China, resembled a mighty dragon crossing China from east to west. Very little of this original wall remains standing or intact.

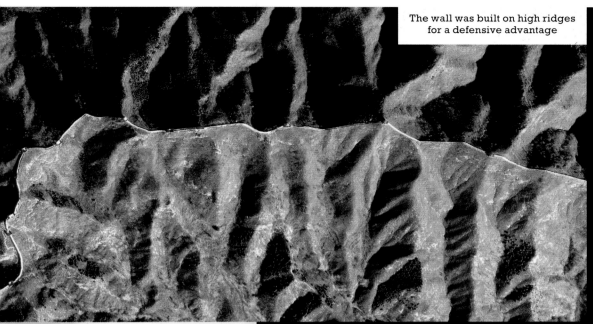

The wall was built on high ridges for a defensive advantage

Walled kingdoms

From 453 BCE, China was divided into several warring kingdoms that each built earthworks and walls to protect their territory. In 221 BCE, Qin Shi Huang united the kingdoms and ordered that the walls be joined and extended to provide a defensive barrier against Huns in the north.

Watch towers

These were built, often of brick, along the wall at regular intervals as lookout posts and fortresses. Bricks quickened construction, as local materials could be used in their making and they were small and light to handle. Kilns to bake the bricks were built alongside the wall.

A brick watch tower with far-reaching views

Building materials

Early sections of the wall were made with compacted earth and wood. Bricks, tiles, and a lime mortar were used during the Ming era.

Strong as stone

Most early sections of the wall have gone, but the later repairs using stone were more durable.

In **2009**, **111 miles** (180 km) of **wall** were **discovered** using **infrared sensors** and **GPS** devices.

The breathtaking section at Jiankou

Protection and repair

Some sections are in good condition, such as the section at Badaling, built in the Ming Dynasty and the first to open to tourists in 1957. However, many sections require protection and restoration. The China Great Wall Society is dedicated to the mapping, conservation, and documentation of the wall.

Sahara Desert

The Sahara is the **largest** hot desert in the world and covers most of north Africa. It is famous for its sand **dunes**, but it actually contains almost every kind of desert **terrain**, from rocky plateau to plant-filled **scrubland**. The air in the Sahara contains almost no moisture and the **mountains** between the desert and the coast prevent **clouds** and any rain to reach the center. The Sahara stretches from the Atlantic Ocean in the west to the **Red Sea** in the east. It is the **third** largest desert after Antarctica and the Arctic, and its name means **"Greatest Desert"** in Arabic.

Facts and figures

Protected sites
In 1992, the Air and Ténéré Natural Reserves in the middle of the Sahara were designated World Heritage Sites. These areas contain a variety of plants, landscapes, and animals.

Rainfall
In the center and east of the desert, the average annual rainfall is virtually nonexistent. The rest of the Sahara gets less than 20 mm.

Size
The Sahara stretches roughly 3,000 miles (4,800 km) from east to west and 1,110 miles (1,800 km) from north to south.

Dunes
Some of the sand dunes are 600 ft (180 m) high.

Temperature extremes
On winter nights, the temperature can drop below freezing, but daytime temperatures can reach 116°F (47°C).

The Sahara is a place of extremes — blistering hot days, freezing cold nights.

Desert growth

The Sahara is expanding. It is now more than 154,440 sq miles (400,000 sq km) bigger than it was in 1957. This is called desertification.

No place like home

Only two million people call the Sahara home. People in this part of the world are nomads. Instead of living in a house, they move from place to place to find food and water.

The Tuareg people use camels because of their speed and stamina

Did you know?

The USA could fit easily inside the Sahara. The countries Algeria, Chad, Egypt, Eritrea, Libya, Morocco, Niger, Mali, Mauritania, the Sudan, and Tunisia are all part of the desert.

Waw an Namus is an oasis in a volcanic field in the Sahara

Other big deserts

A desert is any area of land where there is little rainfall per year, making it hard for many plants and animals to survive. They are not necessarily hot places.

Antarctic
The Antarctic is considered a desert because of its low rainfall (this falls as snow). It covers a larger area than the Sahara Desert.

Kalahari Desert
This savannah covers parts of Botswana, South Africa, and Namibia. More animals live here than is possible in a sand desert.

Lost oases

Thousands of years ago, the Sahara was a lush, green place where people could grow crops. Now, plants can only grow when underground rivers bubble to the surface. Oases account for about two percent of the Sahara Desert.

Shifting sand

Dunes are hills made out of sand that are created and changed by the wind. The sand dunes of the Sahara cover an area of more than 3,862 sq miles (10,000 sq km). The dunes do not stay still—they are constantly moved by the wind. A desert storm can shift a dune hundreds of feet and bury whole cities. Many ancient cities are buried under the desert.

This caravan city on the fringe of the Sahara was buried by sand

Animals of the desert

The Sahara Desert doesn't offer a life of luxury, but some creatures do manage to live there. Dung beetles, camels, scorpions, sidewinder snakes, gazelles, and antelopes are among the animals that make their home in the sand. There are also around 500 plant species in the center of the Sahara.

Salar de Uyuni
The world's largest salt flat is in Bolivia, 12,000 ft (3,656 m) above sea level. It is covered by a crust of salt several feet thick.

An adult scorpion in western Sahara

9

Victoria Falls

Victoria Falls is the world's **largest** waterfall, with the entire width of the **Zambezi** River dropping 354 ft (108 m) into a chasm before being channeled through a series of **gorges**. It lies between Zimbabwe and Zambia in southern **Africa**, and many fish, birds, and mammals make it home. There are several tree-covered **islands** in the river, and some of these islands divide the **water** into streams as it drops over the falls. Rainbows and **moonbows** often form above the water, and the thunderous **noise** and mist give the falls its local name: Mosi-oa-Tunya—Smoke that **Thunders**.

Facts and figures

Natural wonder
Victoria Falls was designated a World Heritage Site in 1989 and is one of the Seven Natural Wonders of the World.

Still changing
Water is still changing the face of the falls. A new precipice is slowly being eroded away.

Gorges
There are six main gorges. One contains a power station.

Measurements
Victoria Falls is 5,604 ft (1,708 m) wide and 354 ft (108 m) high. It is arguably the largest combination of height, width, and volume of flow.

Ancient stones
Artifacts like digging tools, weapons, and jewelry show that early humans may have lived here three million years ago. There is also evidence of Middle Stone Age settlements.

Did you know?

The spray of water that rises from Victoria Falls can be seen up to 30 miles (48 km) away. It usually gets to 1,300 ft (400 m), but it can reach double that height.

Victoria Falls is the widest single curtain of water in the world

The world's largest sheet of falling water is twice the height of Niagara Falls.

Out of sight
During the rainy season, you can't see the base of the falls or even its face because of the constant mist and spray.

Lunar rainbows
During a full moon, a spray "moonbow" is created over the falls. It is made by light reflecting off the surface of the moon, and is paler than a daytime rainbow.

Volume of water

In April, when peak flood waters occur, the flow is an estimated 625 million liters of water per minute. The powerful roar of the water can be heard 12 miles (20 km) away. The water level is lowest at the end of the dry winter period in October and November. On the Zambian side—the eastern end—the water can sometimes dry up completely.

Falls formation

The plateau over which the river flows is made of basalt rock, but long cracks in the basalt are filled with soft sandstone. Over thousands of years, the sandstone was worn away by the constant flow of water, creating the 8 miles (13 km) of gorges we see today.

The highest-ever flow was recorded in 1958

The zigzagging Batoka Gorges

River animals

There are two national parks beside the falls, and several more along the banks of the Zambezi. The river contains many fish, hippos, and crocodiles, and supports owls, eagles, otters, and herons. Splash from the waterfall creates a "rain forest" environment and, in the dry season, elephants cross the river.

Hippos are some of the most dangerous animals in Africa

Fact file

Huge waterfalls

Victoria Falls is just one of many famous waterfalls that have been discovered. Here are some other spectacular cascades from around the world.

Detian Falls

These two waterfalls straddle the border between China and Vietnam. Many species of plants are only found here.

Ouzoud Falls

There are many projects to help protect these falls in Morocco. They are 330 ft (110 m) high and have three separate drops.

King George Falls

These falls in Kimberley, Australia, are often viewed from boats. The water flow is most powerful between December and May.

Petra

This **ancient** city is located in Jordan, in the Middle East. It is surrounded by mountain passes and deep **twisting** gorges, and was carved right into the **sandstone** cliffs by the Nabatean people. The main entrance is through the **Siq**, a narrow gorge with sheer cliff walls up to 650 ft (200 m) high. Inside are **hundreds** of structures, including an **elaborate** temple called the Treasury. Petra was absorbed into the Roman **Empire** in 106 CE and was an **important** trading city. It was damaged by an earthquake in 363 CE, which led to the eventual **desertion** of the city.

Facts and figures

Heritage site
The city has been a World Heritage Site since 1985.

Nabateans
The Nabateans were Arabic people, and Petra may have been established as early as 312 BCE as the capital city of their kingdom.

Inspirational
John William Burgon's famous poem described Petra as "a rose-red city half as old as Time."

Discovery
Locals led explorer Johann Burckhardt to Petra in 1812. This city had been lost to the world for 1,000 years.

The Treasury's name
This building is not a bank, it is a tomb. It was named because of the legend that the urn at the top of the facade contained a treasure.

Size
The city covers 102 sq miles (264 sq km).

The Treasury was built at the beginning of the 1st century CE

Lost beauty

Inscriptions may have been on the facades of many of the buldings, which were once covered in plaster and paint. But only a few inscriptions have been found.

Plain and simple

Behind the Treasury's impressive facade, there is only a square, blank chamber hewn from sandstone, with smaller rooms leading from it.

Did you know?

Petra is also known as the Rose City because of the rose-red sandstone, but some rocks and cave walls display swirling bands and streaks in a rainbow of colors.

Petra is the Greek word for rock.

Cave dwellings set within the rock face

City of tombs

There are many tombs in this city. Some of the most elaborate of these are known as the Royal Tombs. Because so few inscriptions have been found, no one knows for whom they were built. The thousands of carved rock caves would have been homes for the people who lived there.

A slow decline

The Roman Empire absorbed the area in 106 CE. At first, Petra continued to thrive. However, over the following centuries, Arabian trade moved away from the city and Petra declined. The last occupants abandoned the city in 663 CE, when the Arabs conquered the region.

A Roman amphitheater with tombs in the rock wall behind it

Wear and tear

Parts of Petra suffer from erosion because of strong winds and increasing tourism.

Mud houses

Most homes in Petra would have been made of mud bricks, and therefore disappeared hundreds of years ago.

Intricate aqueducts brought water to the city's fountains

Vital water provision

A system for storing and supplying water made it possible for 30,000 people to live in Petra. In an arid desert area, that is impressive—there was even enough water for lush gardens. The settlement also used dams and channels to control the flash floods that often cut through the gorges.

Taj Mahal

India's Taj Mahal, with its large white dome and four **minarets,** is one of the most **recognized** buildings in the world. It isn't a palace—it is a **mausoleum**, a building that houses the tomb of a deceased person. It was built for **Emperor** Shah Jahan's wife, who died in 1631, as a **shrine** to his love for her. It also showed off his wealth. Thousands of **craftsmen** worked on the building between 1632 and 1654. It lies on the River **Yamuna**, near the city of Agra. **Marble** was transported 180 miles (300 km) to build the mausoleum, which was **decorated** with precious stones.

The **Taj Mahal** is **regarded** as the "**jewel** of **Muslim art in India.**"

Facts and figures

UNESCO
The Taj Mahal was designated a World Heritage Site in 1983.

Awe-inspiring
The central marble building is topped by a large dome and a feature called a finial. The finial is 15 ft (4.6 m) high.

Tourists
Every year, between seven and eight million people visit Agra to see the Taj Mahal.

Height
The Taj Mahal is 240 ft (73 m) high. The dome is 115 ft (35 m) high.

Golden triangle
This is the tourist circuit of Delhi, Agra, and Jaipur. Jaipur and Delhi also contain several World Heritage Sites.

Garden
The Taj Mahal gardens show respect to the Shah's religion, Islam, that regards gardens as a symbol of paradise.

Yellow-billed stork walk in the Yamuna River next to the Taj Mahal

Did you know?

Mumtaz was only one of Shah Jahan's wives, but she was his favorite. He was devastated when she died during childbirth. Shah Jahan is buried in the Taj Mahal alongside his wife.

Truth or legend?

Most historians believe the Taj Mahal was built by Shah Jahan's 20,000 craftsmen. However, some think it was built centuries earlier as a temple, and only added to by Shah Jahan.

His and hers

It is said that Shah Jahan planned a matching black marble mausoleum for himself, but his rule ended before it could be built.

In the light of early morning the Taj Mahal is a soft pink-red color

It turns milky white as the sun sets and golden in moonlight

Fact file

Other tombs

A mausoleum is more than a tomb. It is an impressive building that honors the dead and contains the burial chamber. They were often built for leaders.

Castel Sant'Angelo
This round tomb in Italy, later used as a fortress, was the final resting place of Emperor Hadrian and other Roman emperors.

Terracotta Army
The mausoleum of the first emperor of China included 8,000 life-size terracotta warrior sculptures to protect him in the afterlife.

Shah-i-Zinda
This necropolis, or cemetery, in Uzbekistan was built for royals and nobles, and contains rows of mosaic-covered tombs.

Intricate marble carvings on a wall

Colors

The Taj Mahal's beautiful marble looks different according to the time of day and the light. The marble absorbs and reflects light to create varied colors, and these may symbolize the presence of Allah, the Arabic word for God.

Carvings

Religious Islamic art is not allowed to show Allah's creations, like humans and animals. Instead, verses from the Quran adorn the walls, using words and letters to create patterns. The white marble is inlaid with many precious stones and black marble. The 99 names of Allah are beautifully inscribed on the sides of Mumtaz's tomb.

Thefts and threats

Over time, irreplaceable items, such as silver doors, gold railings, and the cloth of pearls that draped over Mumtaz's tomb, have been stolen from the Taj Mahal. There was a plan in the 1830s to sell off the marble piece by piece. Today, the threats are acid rain, air pollution, and the traffic of millions of tourists.

Air pollution and acid rain are a threat to the marble

Angkor Wat

Angkor Wat, in southeast **Asia**, is the largest religious monument in the world. It lies deep within the Cambodian **jungle** on a rectangular **island** surrounded by a wide moat. It contains the remains of several capital **cities** built between the 9th and 15th centuries. A significant part of it was built as a **Hindu** temple and a capital city, Angkor Thom, by **King** Suryavarman II in the 12th century. There are **hundreds** of temples and thousands of stone carvings. It fell out of use in the 1430s after attacks by the **Thai** empire, but in the 1970s refugees took **shelter** here from the civil war.

Facts and figures

World Heritage Site
Angkor Wat was made a UNESCO World Heritage Site in 1992.

Super size
The outer wall is 3,360 ft (1,024 m) long and 2,600 ft (800 m) high. The moat is 623 ft (190 m) wide.

Western entrance
The main entrance is in the western wall. West is the direction of death in Hindu, so Angkor Wat may have had use as a funeral temple.

Sandstone
The stone used to build Angkor Wat came from a holy mountain called Phnom Kulen, 31 miles (50 km) away, and transported along canals.

Nature spirits
Over 3,000 nymphs—mythical characters representing nature—are carved in the walls.

Khmer
The Khmer people are the main ethnic group in Cambodia.

Angkor Wat was once the bustling center of the Khmer kingdom.

The Angkor ruins stretch over more than 248 sq miles (400 sq km)

Did you know?

Angkor Wat was originally a Hindu temple dedicated to Vishnu, but was later cared for by Buddhist monks. It became a Buddhist temple around the 14th century.

Decline of Angkor

In the 15th century, the Khmer kings moved to the coast, where they built Phnom Penh, the capital of Cambodia.

A great king

Angkor Wat means "city of temples" and was Suryavarman II's capital city and state temple. During his reign, he reunited the Khmer empire and built many other temples.

A building dwarfed by strangler figs

Jungle damage

In some places, the roots of strangler figs and banyan trees are growing into Angkor Wat's buildings, which are dangerous to its structure and ancient carvings. Tree roots have grown around, over, under, and through the rock. In some cases, the trees are holding the buildings together. Restoration, conservation, and repair are ongoing.

Carvings

Vivid stone carvings of Hindu scenes, gods and goddesses, as well as real figures, appear in friezes some hundreds of feet long. One of the most famous is the Churning of the Sea of Milk, which shows a creation story from Hindu mythology.

The Churning of the Sea of Milk carving

Home of the gods

The five central sandstone towers are thought to represent the five peaks of Mount Meru, which is the home of the Hindu gods.

Proud country

Angkor Wat is on Cambodia's flag. It is the world's only national flag that includes a building.

Divine kings

The Khmer rulers were believed to be Vishnu embodied in human form. Vishnu is one of the three main Hindu gods. Images of him are usually shown with blue skin and eight arms. Angkor Wat may have been modeled on the Hindu vision of the home of the gods. It is visited today by many pilgrims.

Buddhists gave this statue of Vishnu the head of Buddha

Giant's Causeway

The Giant's Causeway lies at the foot of basalt **cliffs** along the northern Irish **coast**, and was declared a national nature reserve in 1987. It is easy to imagine how the **legend** of the causeway being a path for **giants** arose; the 40,000 interlocking pillars look like stepping stones that run from the cliffs and out into the **sea**. Around 50–60 million years ago, **lava** flowed from inside the Earth, then cooled and hardened into straight-sided, flat-topped **basalt** columns. This **inspiring** site on the shores of the North Channel is one of Northern Ireland's most iconic **natural** landmarks.

This **natural landscape** looks **man-made** and has **fascinated** **people** for **centuries.**

Facts and figures

Recognition
It has been a UNESCO World Heritage Site since 1986.

In numbers
The average height of the cliffs is 330 ft (100 m). The tallest columns are up to 82 ft (25 m) in height and 15–20 in (38–51 cm) in diameter.

Force of nature
Giant's Causeway was voted in 2005 as the fourth greatest natural wonder in the UK.

Eminent owners
Part of the Giant's Causeway is owned and managed by the National Trust and part is owned by private individuals. The rest belongs to the Crown Estate, which means that the reigning UK monarch is the legal owner.

Hidden for years
About 15,000 years ago, after the last Ice Age, the columns were exposed at the shore.

Did you know?
This rock formation near the causeway is the Giant's Organ Pipes. They are so-named because the tall, thin basalt columns resemble the pipes of a church organ.

Most of the basalt columns have between five and seven sides

Tight fitting
Many of the columns fit so closely together that it is impossible to insert as much as the blade of a knife between them.

Nature's creations
Partial weathering of basalt blocks has left colored circles around a central nugget of basalt. Local people know them as the "giant's eyes."

Lava flowing into the sea

Causeway formation

Around 50–60 million years ago, this area experienced volcanic activity. Molten rock (lava) from inside the Earth was forced to the surface, where it cooled and hardened into a plateau. As the rapidly cooling lava contracted, differences in the cooling rate led to the formation of the columns.

Amazing shapes

Several of the rocks in this area have been eroded over millions of years and now resemble other objects. As well as the Organ Pipes, there is the Giant's Boot, the Giant's Harp, the Chimney Stacks, the Honeycomb, the Shepherd's Steps, the Giant's Gate, and the Camel's Hump.

McCool legend

When Scottish giant Benandonner annoyed Irish giant Finn McCool, Finn threw chunks of coast into the sea as a path to Scotland. But Benandonner was massive! Finn hid, disguised as a baby. The Scot knew that if this was Finn's baby, its father must be colossal. He fled, destroying the causeway.

The Giant's Boot, left behind by Finn, is 5 ft (150 cm) tall

Finn's causeway would have to be 22 miles (35 km) long to reach Scotland

Grand Canyon

This vast gorge in northern **Arizona**, USA, was carved out by the **Colorado** River millions of years ago. The canyon, shaped by the river and the **weather**, now cuts across the Grand Canyon National Park. Its beautifully preserved **geologic** record tells the story of the **Earth** over almost two billion years. The area has been inhabited by Native Americans for **thousands** of years, and the first recorded **European** visitor arrived in 1540 seeking the Seven Cities of **Gold**. The Grand Canyon was designated a US National Monument in 1908 by **President** Theodore Roosevelt.

The Grand Canyon was formed over six million years

The layers of rock in the Grand Canyon's cliffs tell the story of how it was formed.

Dizzy heights

The depth of the canyon is breathtaking. From the top of the canyon looking down, the Colorado River is about 4900 ft (1.5 km) below.

Water's journey

The river flows west through the Grand Canyon and travels at an average speed of 3.7 miles (6 km) per hour. Its course was established at least 17 million years ago.

Did you know?

Humans lived here at least 10,500 years ago, and there are artifacts showing that Native American tribes, like the Ancestral Pueblo, lived in the canyon area from 3,000 BCE.

Balance Rock at Lee's Ferry, the official start of the National Park

Fact file

Other canyons

A canyon slices between two cliffs and is formed over a long period of time. Below you will find more impressive and important canyons.

Fish River Canyon
The largest canyon in Africa is found in Namibia. It is a 100-mile (160-km)-long ravine formed from shale, sandstone, and lava.

Verdon Gorge
This 16-mile (25-km)-long gorge in France is one of the most beautiful in Europe, with limestone cliffs that are perfect for rock climbing.

Bryce Canyon
This Utah, USA, canyon boasts hoodoos, or tall spires of rock. These geological wonders are formed by weathering.

Weather erosion

Balance Rock is a mushroom-shaped rock that has formed over thousands of years. The mudstone on which it was resting was eroded from beneath by water and wind. Because wind is at its strongest within 3 ft (1 m) of the ground, the stem of the mushroom weathered faster than the crown.

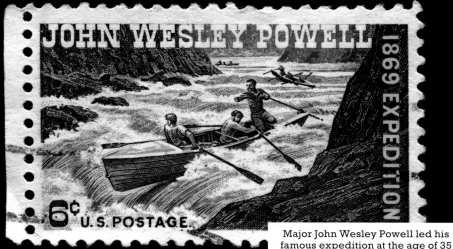

JOHN WESLEY POWELL
1869 EXPEDITION
6¢ U.S. POSTAGE

Major John Wesley Powell led his famous expedition at the age of 35

John Powell

John Wesley Powell was an unusual man who went on collecting and exploring trips. He taught himself botany, zoology, and geology. In 1869, he took nine men to cover almost 930 miles (1,500 km) through uncharted canyons. Three months later, he returned from the Grand Canyon with five survivors.

Formation

Millions of years ago, the powerful Colorado River cut a channel through the limestone, sandstone, shale, granite, and schist rock layers. Erosion of these layers continues today. The North Rim, almost 1,000 ft (300 m) higher than the South Rim, gets more rain and snow; the South Rim is drier and warmer.

The snow-covered North Rim of the canyon

Mount Rushmore

The enormous **sculptures** carved out of the side of Mount Rushmore in South Dakota, USA, are a modern **wonder**. The sculpture depicts four **American** presidents and was designed to bring **tourists** to the area of the Black Hills. It worked. Two million people each year come to see the "Shrine to **Democracy**." George **Washington**, Thomas Jefferson, Theodore Roosevelt, and Abraham **Lincoln** all made vital contributions to the first 130 years of American history after **independence**. In 1939, the last head was dedicated and Mount Rushmore **opened** in 1941.

Facts and figures

Cost
The sculptures cost one million dollars.

New name
The Native Americans called the mountain Six Grandfathers. It was renamed Mount Rushmore in 1885, after a New York lawyer.

Secret vault
There is a chamber hidden behind the faces, containing 16 panels of information about American history.

Huge statesmen
The faces are 60 ft (18 m) high and the whole memorial covers 2 sq mi (5.17 sq km). It stands 5,725 ft (1,745 m) above sea level.

Explosive work
About 450,000 tons of rock were blown off the face of the mountain.

Health and safety
It was unusual for a project of this size that no one died during the carving process.

It **took** 14 years to **complete** the Mount Rushmore **sculptures.**

Left to right: George Washington, Thomas Jefferson, Theodore Roosevelt, and Abraham Lincoln

Did you know?

The original plan was to portray the presidents from head to waist, as shown in Borglum's model. However, funding ran out before the full sculptures could be completed.

Sun gazers

Mount Rushmore was chosen partly because the cliff faces southeast, and therefore gets as much sunlight as possible.

Order of presidents

Jefferson was originally planned to appear on Washington's right, but the rock was not suitable for carving, and the figure had to be sculpted on Washington's left instead.

Crazy Horse is still far from being finished

Native Americans

The Mount Rushmore sculptures are controversial because this region is considered by many to rightfully belong to Native Americans. On a nearby mountainside, an even bigger sculpture is being made of Crazy Horse, a Native American warrior. Work started in 1948.

Years of work

To start work on Rushmore, dynamite was used to blast the granite. Then, 400 masons started chiseling, following the sculptor's designs. Work was interrupted many times by bad weather and lack of money. It is estimated that during the 14-year period, only 6½ years' work was done.

Huge sculptures

For centuries, mankind has created larger-than-life figures for art, honor, and worship. There are many magnificent sculptures around the globe.

Statue of Liberty
Situated in New York Harbor, this statue, a symbol of freedom, was a gift to America from France in 1886. It is made of copper.

Scaffolds enabled the masons to do their work

Christ the Redeemer
This statue, clad in mosaic tiles, is 100 ft (30 m) high and overlooks Rio de Janeiro, Brazil. Its arms span 92 ft (28 m).

Gutzon Borglum

Borglum was a Danish-American sculptor who trained in Paris. He was 60 when he started work on the Mount Rushmore sculptures, which occupied him until he died unexpectedly in 1941. After his death, his son, Lincoln Borglum, continued the project until a lack of funding forced construction to end.

The heads can be seen from several miles away

Avukana Buddha statue
This 39 ft (12 m) statue of the Buddha is in Sri Lanka. It was carved in the 5th century from an enormous boulder of granite.

Machu Picchu

Machu Picchu is perched between two **mountains**, high above the **Urubamba** River in Peru, South America. It is thought to have been built in the 15th century by the **Inca** people, and opinions differ as to its purpose. There are many gardens, **terraces**, palaces, and **ceremonial** buildings. Different levels are connected by steps and there are also **aqueducts**, fountains, and baths. After it was abandoned in the mid-1500s, it became **lost** to the jungle. It was rediscovered in **1911** showing little damage, and is one of the world's most famous **archaeological** sites.

Did you know?

American historian Hiram Bingham revealed Machu Picchu to the world in 1911. While he was searching for the lost city of the Incas, local people led him to these spectacular ruins.

This **dramatic and mysterious city** is **high** in the **Andes Mountains.**

Machu Picchu (old peak) is overlooked by Huayna Picchu (young peak)

Many mysteries

How many people lived here? How was each building used? Could this have been a temple, a royal retreat, a university? No one can be certain.

Food and drink

Maize, potatoes, and other crops were grown on the terraced hillside. The water came from springs and was carried by stone drains to the crops, ponds, fountains, and baths.

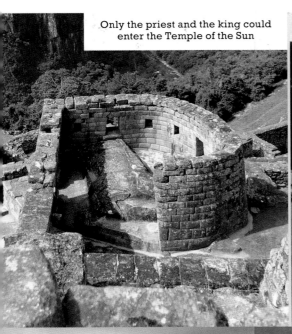

Only the priest and the king could enter the Temple of the Sun

It was believed that the Inti Watana stone held the sun in place in the sky

Sun worship

The Inca people dedicated many ceremonies to Inti, their sun god. The Inti Watana stone points at the sun during the winter solstice and is sometimes called "The Hitching Post of the Sun." The Temple of the Sun, where only important rituals were held, is on the city's highest point.

Quarried rock

Modern machines can now cut granite, but incredibly the Incas worked with it, even without iron tools. They may have inserted wet wooden wedges into holes in the rock, waited for the water to freeze, then split the rock. The quarry from which the granite came can still be seen.

The quarry sits just on the edge of the mountain

Inca Trail Race

This mountainous marathon—the world's hardest—with thousands of steps ends at Machu Picchu.

Clever technique

The stones are cut so accurately that nothing can fit between them. They "dance" during an earthquake then fall back into place.

Condor altar

The Temple of the Condor is an example of skillful Inca stonemasonry. They shaped a natural rock formation into the spreading wings of a condor in flight. On the floor of the temple, a rock is carved into the shape of a condor's head and neck feathers, completing the figure of the bird.

The condor's head may have been used as a sacrificial altar

Galapagos Islands

The Galapagos Islands, nearly 620 miles (1,000 km) off the **coast** of Ecuador, South America, are famous for their **unique** flora and fauna. The area has been called "a living museum." The first islands **formed** here at least eight **million** years ago and were visited by British naturalist **Charles Darwin** on his voyage on the HMS *Beagle* in 1835. Darwin found that these **islands**, cut off from the rest of the world, had **species** of birds, animals, and plants that were found nowhere else on Earth. His **findings** helped him to formulate his ideas about natural selection and **evolution**.

Facts and figures

UNESCO
The islands were designated a World Heritage Site in 1978.

Broad area
The total land area of the Galapagos Islands is 3,090 sq mi (8,010 sq km), across 23,000 sq mi (59,500 sq km) of ocean.

Protected
The islands are surrounded by the Galapagos Marine Reserve, which is the same size as Greece.

Wildlife sanctuary
Since 1959, 97% of the archipelago has been a national park.

For animals
There are 127 islands, islets, and rocks. But only four islands (3% of the total) are inhabited by humans.

First name
In 1535, the Bishop of Panama discovered the islands and named them Las Encantadas, "The Enchanted."

Parts of the island's 840 miles (1,350 km) of coastline suffered in a 2011 tsunami.

Pinnacle Rock on Bartolomé, one of the Galapagos islands

Did you know?

In the last 200 years, there have been over 50 volcanic eruptions here. Each island was formed from a volcano growing from the seabed, apart from Isabela, which is made up of six volcanoes.

Isabela
San Salvador
Santa Cruz
Fernandina
San Cristóbal
Floreana

Wolf Volcano

Wolf Volcano erupted in 2015 for the first time in 33 years. Gas and ash shot up 9 miles (15 km). Incredibly, the animals on the island were unharmed.

Island climate

As well as the distinct rainy and dry seasons, a change in the ocean currents, called El Nino, periodically brings heavy rain, causing floods, landslides, and affecting animal life.

A cactus-eating Darwin finch on a prickly pear

Distinctive finches

The 13 species of finch on the islands probably evolved from one common species. Each species has a different beak shape and size that best suits what it eats. Cactus-eating finches have large beaks shaped for getting seeds out of cacti, while warbler finches have thin, sharp beaks for spearing insects.

Fact file

Unusual animals

An amazing range of unusual animals can be found on these islands. They attract 170,000 tourists and many researchers every year.

Galapagos tortoise
The world's largest tortoise can live up to 150 years. There were 15 different types, but four are now extinct.

Charles Darwin

In 1859, Darwin published his theory of evolution in *On Origin of the Species*. He used evidence he had gathered during his explorations, including his findings from the Galapagos Islands. He set out to explain how he thought animals and plants evolved over time by natural selection.

Marine iguanas

These are the only lizards that can live in the sea. They can dive up to 100 ft (30 m) and hold their breath for 45 minutes. They are brightly colored during the mating season but a darker shade the rest of the year. The dark color helps these cold-blooded reptiles absorb heat from the sun.

Darwin's famous ship, the HMS *Beagle*

Galapagos cormorant
The only cormorant to have lost its ability to fly. Its webbed feet propel it to the seabed to feed on fish, eels, and small octupuses.

Galapagos penguin
This is the second smallest penguin species in the world and the only one to live north of the equator. The average length is 19 in (49 cm).

The marine iguana has partially webbed feet

Great Barrier Reef

Australia's Great Barrier Reef is the **largest** single structure made by **living** things. It is composed of thousands of coral reefs, with many small islands, atolls, and **lagoons**, and can even be seen from **space**. The reef stretches along the northeastern coast of Australia where the waters are **warm** and shallow. The reef is home to a great diversity of life; thousands of different species of **fish** and shellfish live here and hundreds of different **birds** and corals. The reef we see today is between **6,000** and **8,000** years old, and it is **visited** by more than two millon tourists and divers a year.

Facts and figures

Universal value
The Great Barrier Reef became a World Heritage Site in 1981.

Vast area
It is over 1,242 miles (2,000 km) long and covers about 134,000 sq mi (348,000 sq km) —bigger than the UK, Holland, and Switzerland combined.

Bird life
There are 215 bird species that visit or roost on reef islands.

Diversity
The reef contains 1,500 types of fish, 400 types of coral, 500 species of seaweed, and 4,000 species of mollusk.

Islands
There are more than 900, from small, sandy cays to large islands.

Big and small
The smallest fish in the reef is a mere ¼ in (7 mm) long, and the largest can grow to a length of 33 ft (10 m).

The vastness of this colorful, intricate ecosystem is best seen from the air.

Reefs grow an average of half an inch (1.3 cm) every year

Did you know?

One of the creatures found living on the reef is a mollusk called the chambered nautilus. It is the largest species of nautilus, and it lives where the reef slopes down into deep water.

Dating the reef

Coral deposits have been discovered that date back half a million years. The new reef grew on top of the old reef.

Variety of life

Some people call coral reefs the "rain forests of the ocean." They are second only to tropical rain forests in terms of the number of species found in one area.

Types of reef

A barrier reef grows parallel to the coastline, but is separated from it by deep, wide lagoons. The other classes of reef are rings of coral called atolls; fringing reefs that grow close to the shore; and small, isolated patch reefs. The Great Barrier Reef is the best-known barrier reef in the world.

Coral polyps

These primitive animals live in large groups and have a soft body covered by a skeleton of hard limestone. Their skeletons make up the reef. A living reef takes thousands of years to form, mostly out of empty skeletons that are used by other life forms, such as sponges, sea slugs, oysters, and clams.

Lady Musgrave Island is a coral atoll

Colorful, healthy coral in its natural habitat

Reef in danger

There are many threats to the future of the reef, some natural and some man-made. They include debris from shipping accidents, oil spills, pollution by tourists, over-fishing, and coral bleaching. The crown of thorns starfish is highly dangerous because it feeds on coral polyps, sucking the life from the reef.

Human threats: a ship leaks oil on the reef

Fact file

Weird creatures

The Great Barrier Reef is home to many wonderfully weird animals, like the dugong and nautilus, but here are perhaps three of its oddest inhabitants.

Nudibranch
With no shell protection, this tough-skinned sea slug uses toxic secretions and stingers to defend its colorful body.

Christmas tree worm
This worm has two spirals of tentacles, shaped like Christmas trees, which catch prey and carry it to the worm's mouth.

Cuttlefish
This relation of the squid has a shell inside its body, eight arms, and W-shaped pupils. It can change its skin color at will.

Rotorua

In the **heart** of New Zealand's North Island is an extraordinary area with more than 1,000 **geothermal** features: geysers, mud pools, hot **springs,** and mineral pools. The city of Rotorua is a popular destination with tourists, with **tourism** being the largest and most **important** industry in the district. Rotorua is a place that is rich in **Māori** history and culture. Most of the lakes around the city have formed due to **volcanic** activity. The colors of the lakes and shores come from naturally present **minerals**—iron **oxide** turns shorelines red, and white sulphur makes them yellow.

Facts and figures

Attractions
Rotorua has 18 lakes and three major rivers. Some lakes are sacred to the Māori people. It also has around 500 hot springs and the largest geyser in the country.

Lost wonder
The shores of Lake Rotomahana once boasted the stunning Pink and White Terraces. However, they were destroyed when Mount Tarawera erupted in 1886.

Kakahi Falls
This is the southern hemisphere's largest hot waterfall. At 104°F (40°C), it is the temperature of a nice hot shower!

Size
Tikitapu is the smallest of the lakes; Rotorua is the largest.

Varying temperatures
Champagne Pool stays at 163°F (73°C), while the water in Inferno Pool is over 212°F (100°C).

Daily eruptions

Named after the daughter of a New Zealand governor, Lady Knox Geyser is induced to erupt at 10:15 a.m. every day, sending water up to 65 ft (20 m) into the air for over an hour.

Big geyser

Pohutu, meaning "explosion," is the main geyser of the area. It spouts every 20 minutes and the jets of water can reach heights of 100 ft (30 m).

Rotorua lies in the depression of a collapsed volcano.

Did you know?

Rotorua's nickname is "Sulphur City" because of its smell of rotten eggs caused by the hydrogen sulfide emissions. It is sometimes called "Rotten-rua" for the same reason.

The amazing colors of the bubbling Champagne Pool

Māori people

The native people of New Zealand, the Māoris, used the geothermal features for cooking, washing, and heating. They also believed that the waters had healing properties for conditions like arthritis and rheumatism. Nowadays, the area is still visited for its spas and healing waters.

Māoris in 1915 using hot springs for cooking

Lady Knox Geyser has an eruption every day, triggered by soap flakes

Pohutu in Te Puia is the largest geyser in the southern hemisphere

How geysers work

A geyser is a spring that ejects water and steam into the air. Water seeps through the ground and is boiled by magma-heated rock. The water rises back to the surface through cracks and vents before erupting from the Earth. When the remaining water in the geyser cools, the eruption stops.

Orakei Korako

The Māori name of this geothermal field means "Place of Adorning." Silica terraces, the largest since the destruction of the Pink and White Terraces in 1886, form the base. As much as 5.3 million gallons (20 million l) of silica-enriched water may flow over the terraces and into Lake Ohakuri every day.

Orakei Korako, the largest geyser field in New Zealand

Fact file

Earth's power

Geothermal energy is clean and sustainable heat produced by molten rock inside the Earth. Here are three more geothermal wonders of the world.

Yellowstone Park

This US national park is based on an active super volcano. Old Faithful, one of 300 geysers, spits out water every 90 minutes.

Valley of Geysers

Together with five other sites in the Kamchatka Peninsula, Russia, this beautiful valley has World Heritage status.

Yellow Dragon Gully

This World Heritage Site in China is known for its colorful pools formed by calcite deposits. It is also home to the giant panda.

Acid rain
Rain made acid by pollution in the air.

Amphitheater
An open circular building with a central "stage" surrounded by seating.

Aqueduct
A channel with sides to carry water.

Archaeology
The study of ancient societies and objects.

Archipelago
A group of islands in a stretch of water.

Artifacts
Objects made by humans.

BCE
Before the Common Era (was BC), covering from year 1 BCE and counting backward to prehistory.

CE
Common Era (was AD), covering from year 1 CE to the current year and into the future.

Century
A period of 100 years.

Chamber
An enclosed space inside a building.

Compacted earth
A mixture of sand, clay, soil, and other materials rammed or pounded to make a building material.

Desert
An arid region—not always hot—where little grows because of zero or minimal rainfall.

Desertification
The process that turns an area into a desert.

Diversity
A location that contains many different life forms.

Dome
A rounded "roof" with a circular base on the top of a building.

Dynasty
A series of rulers from the same family who govern a region or country.

Earthwork
A large bank of soil constructed as a defense in ancient times.

Evolution
The process of how organisms develop from earlier organisms.

Facade
The front of a building.

Finial
An ornament at the top of a roof or wall.

Fortress
A building containing soldiers and military defense equipment.

Frieze
A band of carved or painted decoration.

Geothermal
Heat produced by the internal heat of the Earth.

Heritage
Something left behind by previous generations.

Khufu
Ancient Egyptian pharaoh who died in 2566 BCE.

Lagoon
A body of water separated from an ocean or sea by a sandbank or reef.

Legend
A story, usually very old, that cannot be proven to be true.

Mausoleum
A building containing a tomb or many tombs.

Minaret
A slender tower.

Monument
A statue or building erected to the memory of a notable person or event.

Moonbow
A "rainbow" produced by light from the moon.

Mortar
A cement-like mixture that is used to bond building blocks together.

Mosaic
A picture or pattern created with many pieces of tile or stone.

Naturalist
A person who studies the natural world.

Natural selection
A process that makes an organism better suited to its environment.

Necropolis
Meaning "city of the dead," it is a large cemetery.

Oasis (oases, plural)
A fertile place in a desert.

Pyramid
A structure with three or four sloping sides that meet at the top.

Quarry
A place from which stone is extracted.

Restoration
Returning an object to its original condition.

Savannah
A grassy area with widely spaced trees.

Sphinx
An imaginary creature with the body of an animal and the head of a person.

Stonemason
A person who can cut and shape stone and build structures with it.

Terrace
A flat area cut into a sloping mountainside on which to grow crops.

Terrain
An area of land with its natural features, like mountains and rivers.

Trapezoidal
A four-sided shape with only two parallel sides.

UNESCO
The United Nations Educational, Scientific and Cultural Organization.

World Heritage Sites
These natural sites and man-made places are regarded as outstanding and they are chosen by an agency of UNESCO.